BY HIS

WE BLOG

By His Grace We Blog

© 2017 Carmen Brown of Married by His Grace

Written by Carmen Brown
Marriedbyhisgrace@gmail.com

Edited by Veronica Benavidez

Cover Design & Publishing Services by Jen Stults
jstults@beingconfidentofthis.com

All scripture quotations are taken from New American Standard (NASB), English Standard Version (ESV), and New Living Translation (NLT) Bible. You may refer to any of those versions for deeper understanding and knowledge of scripture.

All information in By His Grace We Blog is from gaining insight and experience and receive no liability for any dissatisfaction from what is offered within the eBook. However, I am confident you will find the information helpful and full of useful insight.

Reviews

"I purchased *By His Grace We Blog* a few months after I started blogging and I wish it had been available before I began. This book is chock-full of helpful tips and godly inspiration. I'd recommend this book to any Christian who has felt the nudge in his or her spirit to write for His glory. It provides the necessary steps to not only ensure a successful start but will give you the spiritual insight needed for carrying out your own call to ministry."

-Natalie Venegas
Milkandhoneyfaith.com

"After I read *By His Grace We Blog*, I knew it would be a great resource for every Christian writer in whatever blogging stage they are in. I was impressed by Carmen's book because she not only shares the how to's of having a blog, but she speaks straight to the heart of the writer. She gives Godly advice about what she's learned along the way in areas such as how to manage time and make wise decisions for your blog. This ebook is different from all the rest in the market because it is targeted for the Christian writer to help keep the Lord first in your life while learning to blog as a ministry."

-Valerie Murray
ValerieMurray.com

"*By His Grace We Blog*, is a must-have resource for every Christian Blogger. I love the balanced approach of walking through the steps of what's necessary to start a blog; how to manage a blog, and most importantly, how to cultivate your blog into ministry. Understanding why we blog and how we blog through God's grace, really put things in perspective for me. In fact, it changed the way my husband and I write and engage with our readers."

- Timberley Gray
LivingOurPriorities.com

"Carmen is someone I look up to in the Christian Blogging world and I cannot recommend her eBook enough! There is so much wisdom and faith-filled instruction on starting a Christ-centered blog and listening to God's will for you in this eBook that I know you will feel blessed by hearing her words."

- Elaine Sinnott
MilitarywifeafterGod.com

Acknowledgements

I am thankful for the love of Christ and for His grace that has saved me. There are no words to express the gratitude I have for God and His unfailing love. He has given me grace and mercy even in the most undeserving times. I am blessed and honored to have the opportunity to spread the gospel through writing. My prayer is for His presence to continue to dwell in all the Christian Bloggers that are pursuing ministry through blogging.

To my husband who always encourages and uplifts me. I am thankful for your friendship and your leadership. Watching you chase God has been one of my greatest blessings because you never leave me behind.

> *Two are better than one because they have a good return for their labor. For if either of them falls, the one will lift up his companion. But woe to the one who falls when there is not another to lift him up.*
>
> *Ecclesiastes 4:9-12*

Grace Girls, through your encouragement and Christ centered friendship I was able to complete this eBook and prepare for the next like minded blogger that we will soon be working side by side with for the glory of the kingdom.

To my dearest friends that taught me what writing with passion truly is. Natalie and Hannah, thank you!

Contents

Introduction

Do you desire to start a Christian blog? Are you being called to fulfill a ministry the Lord has given you through blogging? Do you need your passion guided into starting a blog?

In **By His Grace We Blog**, you will be guided step by step of how to create a Christian blog based off of biblical principles. Each chapter speaks volumes of experience as blogging tips and tools are shared. You will also learn how to use common social media platforms such as Facebook, Instagram, Pinterest, and Twitter for the benefit of your blog.

When I first started a Christian blog it was hard for me to find a Christian perspective on blogging. There was limited resources of how to begin in the Christian niche. I was curious about topics such as: creating goals, monetizing from a Christian blog, building a business from blogging, branding, how to use social media, and how to network with other bloggers in the same niche as me.

My hope for this book is to share my experience and knowledge so that you will gain encouragement and useful insight. My desire for us as Christian bloggers is to succeed for the purpose of what we have been called, to minister through writing.

"Defining your goals is not just carelessly writing what you think you can achieve with your blog. It's about meditating on the purpose of the blog, the process of creating a blog, the passion you have to develop the blog, the ministry you desire to cultivate through the blog, then roll all of that into small goals that will then develop into your ultimate goals."

-Defining your Goals

After reading this step by step guide of Christian blogging, you will be able to confidently grow as a Christian blogger that is building a ministry and business. The entrepreneurial tips in the guide will increase your insight of what God is able to do for you and your blog through monetizing, through cultivating your ministry and keeping an intimate relationship with the Lord. Every chapter ends with a ***Takeaway Tip*** that will navigate you through the process of a growing business.

– 1 –

Seeking Him First

Before starting a Christian blog, there are a two important things that will need to take place (if you have not done so yet). As someone planning to start a faith based blog, first you will prepare yourself spiritually by knowing the word, being fully confident in your walk with the Lord and having a readiness and alertness to the needs of your readers.

Secondly make sure you are aligned with the Lord by continually and consistently seeking the Lord in all areas of this blog, being content with the calling the Lord has given you and staying within the direction the Lord has been leading you.

Before hitting publish, establishing the conditions above to your blog will be one of the most important moves you will need to do to succeed with your blog.

When reading the testimonies of successful faith based Christian bloggers you will consistently read it is because they heard the calling of the Lord, there was an unction in their soul to spread the gospel and to reach out to people with the Lord's direction.

As you read further into this book I hope you will have discovered this is the same reason why you are about to start this journey of producing a Christian blog; that the Lord gave you the desire and that the Holy Spirit is leading you into this new adventure.

When the Lord first spoke to me about starting a blog, I fought with it. I had concerns with whether this was my personal desire to become a writer or was this truly the Lord leading me into this journey. I did not want the two to conflict and lead to confusion, that is why I myself took the first two steps of spiritually preparing and aligning myself with the Lord.

I dedicated a few months to researching on how to create a blog, best tips of what to do with a blog. I read every "About Me" page from bloggers I enjoyed, I read all reviews of hosting platforms. I read posts from other bloggers and participated in almost every free webinar I came across to learn more about blogging.

Even though all the information I continually took in for over two months paid off and helped me in many ways, I was still not content. Not till the day, I got down on my knees and petitioned to the Lord to give me more clarity. I sought after Him with a heart of wanting to make sure I was doing His will, and not trying to fulfill a dream I once had of becoming a writer.

Within days my husband came to me and said, "It's time." When those words came out of my husband's mouth, the man that I look up to as a leader of our home and the man that I confide in as a help mate, I knew it was time. I then started my blog as we now know as Married by His Grace.

Once, I started seeking God about the blog, things came into place easily, opportunities arose that only would've been by Him. I now received reassurance and confidence in every step of what I was doing because I first went to God about the plans and desires for the blog.

I believe if you knew it was God that inspired you and directed you to have a blog, then you must allow God to lead you in every area of the blog. Seek Him for the name of your blog, seek Him about your topics, seek Him about your writing content.

Seeking Him about your time management and administrative decisions is just as important.

Seeking the Lord first is deeper than just the decision making. It means you are consistently building a relationship with Him of trust and leadership. Your walk should not change to less time with Him than before starting the blog. In contrary, it should become greater. Through blogging you are creating a ministry that will be reaching people in many countries and possibly one day thousands of people. You are now set as an example. Through your blog you represent to all who Christ is. It will become vital not just for your spiritual walk but now for your ministry as a blogger to read your bible, pray and have praise and worship time alone with Him. By the leading of God, your blog is your ministry. Take care of it!

Takeaway Tip: Find a Blog Journal. Purchase a journal that will only be used specifically for your blog. The journal will be to write down your visions, write down your ideas, and prayers for the blog. Keep this journal with you at all times. You never know when an idea for a blog post may come to mind, you will want to write it down. I occasionally write prayers in my blog journal to the Lord of what I hope to accomplish with the blog. By doing this, I gain encouragement and motivation.

– 2 –

Finding Your Niche

When becoming a Christian Blogger you may feel limited to what your specific niche should be. When you hear the title "Christian Blogger", your mind may drift to the thought of only writing about prayer, bible studies, teaching others to raise godly children or how to build a ministry group, and so forth. These are all topics successful Christian Bloggers cover including numerous other topics that is for the purpose of building the kingdom.

Having a Christian based blog is not only about what sounds "Religious" and "Christian-Like". It is about building the foundation of your blog on Christ. Being a Christian blogger is identifying that the purpose of your blog is to glorify God to whomever may read your blog.

Creating a Christ-centered blog does not make it limited, it makes it **valuable**.

Identifying your blog's niche is essential to begin any successful blog. Your niche should be a passion. It should be of something that you are already an expert in and/or will become an expert in because you have the drive to continue learning for your audience.

For example, some bloggers started their blog to keep their families updated with their first home renovations as they worked to complete their dream home. They were consistently learning how to build a home from the foundation up. Once the renovation was over either months or years later, they realized they had developed a passion and even became an expert at DIY home designing and decided to create a publicized blog about DIY and Renovations. From situations just like this; many have become successful. Not because of the niche itself but because they were willing to continue to keep learning and as they became experts they were willing to teach others.

Your learning can not stop. If you stop learning then your readers will stop reading. A reader does not want to read over and over the same DIY project because it's the only one you know. They will want to come back to you and your blog because you taught so well in the first tutorial they read and they liked how you taught through your failures and successes. But they will keep coming back if you have more and more projects to share with them.

Same goes for teaching bible studies on your blog. What did you learn from the bible lesson before you began pouring it out to others? What did God speak to you about it personally in your life? How can you make the bible study become alive over the internet?

The answer is by having a personal learning experience with it. Readers will identify your niche by the passion, expertise and knowledge that you exemplify in your blog.

A niche should be something that comes natural to you. A passion that has been thriving to come out within you. Something that you can talk to your family and friends about for hours.

As a blogger you will need to keep new content coming consistently, so having passion for the topic you choose and a willingness to constantly learn more about your niche is vital for your blog, especially if your plan is to eventually reach a large audience and possibly monetize from your blog.

(Please note: If you are doing this as a hobby or just as an on-line journal that is giving you the opportunity to write your thoughts, prayers, or dreams, then writing without a niche is ok. Finding your niche is for the blogger that is working to monetize from their blog.)

Here are a few questions you can ask yourself to determine what your passion is:

What are some areas others ask for advice or help from you?

What do they believe is your expertise?

What type of blogs do you read? Why do you continue to return to that blog?

What do you want the purpose of your blog to be?

Defining your niche is also about defining your audience. Here are a few questions you should ask yourself to find confidence in determining your niche:

Who are you trying to reach out to? Demographics?

How will your content be helpful to them?

What do you hope your readers will take away from your blog?

Begin to brainstorm in different topics and areas that you feel you are being tugged in and seek the Lord of where He is leading you. Ultimately as a Christian based Blogger you are proclaiming for God to be the leader of the blog. You want to be led by Him not of yourself.

As a follower of Him, we know His thoughts are greater than our thoughts. So let Him lead.

"For my thoughts are not your thoughts, neither are your ways my ways," declares the LORD.   *Isaiah 55:8 NIV*

Takeaway Tip: Draw out a brainstorm plan. Write out three topics you would like to write about. Branch out 3-5 categories from the topics. From the categories, write as many writing contents as you can think of. Which topic brings the most ideas to you? Which topic excites you most as you think of titles for writing contents? This is most likely the topic you will be most passionate writing about.

– 3 –

Before You launch

Before launching a blog there is a lot of preparation. You can easily begin a blog and just go with the flow but I will just assume that if you are reading blogging books like this one then you are hoping to create a blog that will be your brand and develop a following which takes preparation, work, and time to do.

As a subscriber opt-in on Married by His Grace blog, I give a free "30 Things you to do before starting a blog" list. I created this list specifically for new Christian Bloggers. I believe all of them to be important. Here is a list I give to subscribers to my weekly newsletters.

30 Things to do before starting a blog.

1. Before starting this list Pray that God will lead you.

2. Identify your passions. What is your calling and ministry that you can blog about. Golden rule to follow: write about something that you can talk about for hours.

3. Choose your niche. Choosing this before a name is important. This is the whole foundation of your blog. What do you want readers to find there? How do you want to help people with your blog? You can find a list of topics on Marriedbyhisgrace.com blog post "Spreading the Gospel through Blogging."

4. Choose a Domain Name. Check if your desired name for your blog is available. You can do this on Bluehost . Just enter a desired name and you can find out if it is available as a domain name. No more than 69 characters otherwise it will be cut off in search bars.

5. Choose a Tag line. Sweet and Simple. Professional. Short summary of what describes your blog. Suggested to be between 135-160 characters. Meta descriptions will cut off after 160.

6. Decide if the Blog will be part time or full time. Deciding this now will save you a lot of frustration on time management.

7. Write goals. What do you hope to achieve with your blog spiritually? What do you hope to accomplish within a year for yourself and the site?

8. Choose Categories. What topics do you want as main categories that will be on your navigation bar? Example: Faith, Family, Marriage, Bible Study, Youth Group, Music.

9. Choose Sub-Categories. This may not come till you have been writing for a little while and build more content. But is good to have ready.

10. Make a brainstorming page for future posts. Sit down for 15 minutes with no distractions and just write ideas. If you do this before writing you can gain a better understanding of what you truly want to blog about.

11. Write at least 10 posts. This was the best advice I read before starting a blog. When you first start your site, you will spend a lot of time learning and getting it together, so that content sitting on your hard drive will save you time and hassle.

12. Change your mindset that if you start this blog you are now making a brand on all social platforms and on your own site. Most importantly, everything you do, you are representing what you are doing for God's glory. Do not forget that!

13. Clean up your Pinterest boards. You are now making a brand and should look like what your site will represent. This will be time consuming, depending on your amount of existing pins, consider creating a new Pinterest account if needed.

14. Start building Pinterest boards that is in the same niche as your desired blog. Suggested amount of boards is minimum 20 but no more than 50 boards. (This does not include group boards)

15. Buy a planner specifically for blogging. I suggest looking for one you can add notes to for each day of the week. You will continuously learn new things to do for your blog and may have to add to your planner.

16. Purchase a notebook specifically for you to write your blogging ideas in while away from your computer. Find something light and easy to take around with you. (Don't forget a pen.)

17. Purchase the Kindle Book "iBlog - Everything you need to know about blogging from 30 top bloggers". This is a must have if you are truly considering to start a blog about blogging for Christ. It will be the best $5 you will spend towards getting your blog started.

18. Start following 3 bloggers that inspire you in the same niche, sign up for their mailing lists to receive continuous inspiration from them.

19. Start following two bloggers that are not in the same niche you plan to be in but will inspire and motivate you. (The purpose of this is so that you will not only view those in your own

niche, it lessens the opportunity to compare yourself or your vision to bloggers with the same category.)

20. Sign up for newsletters from Simple Pin Media and receive their free Ultimate Pinterest Planner. This planner gives great tips for every month of what to pin and a free stats form to keep track of your own growth. They also send amazing Pinterest tips in their newsletters. This is important because Pinterest will be a marketing tool for your blog.

21. Besides from Pinterest (Pinterest is a must to have as a blogger), pick one other social media you can take time to learn very well. You want to pick one that you will feel comfortable getting on every day to share your content, comment to bloggers, and to build a following and community. Some advice; do not overwhelm yourself with all social medias on top of managing a blog.

22. Twitter - If you have one, start tweeting other bloggers comments about their blog posts and like some Tweets daily.

23. If you have one, make it clean and only in reference to your niche. Remember you are now making a brand.

24. Start posting blogs that inspire you on Facebook. Posting blogs of your favorite bloggers or from ones that have inspired you will help build relationships with other bloggers. It is also important to support your soon to be fellow bloggers. These are the ones that probably once encouraged you, encourage them!

25. Make sure to comment on other blog sites minimum 3 times a week. Continue building a relationship. Find content that inspires you. There is so much to be offered through blog posts to people that take time to read. Remember one day you will hope for someone to do this for you.

26. Sign up for free blogging webinars. There are so many free webinars for beginning bloggers. To learn how to use wordpress, install themes, how to use pinterest as a marketing tool, and so much more! Take advantage of this. It truly made my set up so much easier. Remember if you ever need help, there are so many free resources out there to help a new blogger in technology or how to write content.

27. Start reading and researching about how to start a blog. Do not overwhelm yourself but make sure to educate yourself.

28. Write a letter to yourself why you are starting this blog. Date it. Put it away.

29. Find a new favorite coffee shop to go write at.

30. Pray that God leads you as you begin this journey!

Takeaway Tip: Complete the 30 Things to do before starting a blog list weather you are a new blogger or not. Anything you have not done yet as a blogger that is on this list, begin it today.

– 4 –

Define Your Goals

Defining your goals is not just carelessly writing what you think you can achieve with your blog. It's about meditating on the purpose of the blog, the process of creating a blog, the passion you have to develop the blog, the ministry you desire to cultivate through the blog, then roll all of that into small goals that will then develop into your ultimate goals.

Defining your goals and creating a plan for it will make the impossible to possible and the closer you get to it by achieving one goal at a time, the more realistic the vision will become to you.

All of our ultimate goals are different and will take a different amount of time and process to get to. My dream has always been to write a book. Now here you are reading my first ebook. But my ultimate goal is to write multiple books that will speak volumes about my faith and walk with the Lord. To use my testimonies for His glory and to enrich women's lives with the word of God.

Through blogging I get to achieve this and I have the passion for it but ultimately my goal of writing several books is a process followed by a multitude of completing smaller goals.

By putting deep thought into defining your goals and creating them you are initiating accountability for yourself. Your thoughts are wrapping around the importance of your blog's goals.

Here is an excerpt I read on social media that had been shared thousands of times and I felt I had to share one more time in this part of the book because I believe this one excerpt describes what I hope to relay to you in this chapter. This quote is not just inspirational but it has truth behind it.

> "A dream written down with a date becomes a goal.
> A goal broken down into steps becomes a plan.
> A plan backed by action makes your dreams come true."

As the quote said, the first thing you will want to do is write your goals down.

First I wrote down my ultimate goals for the blog which was aligned with my hope and desire for the blog. Then I created increments of time lines, twelve months, six months, and three months which gave life to my goals.

This works for me. You can choose the increments of time that works for you, just make sure it's attainable and not too far in time or we can get relaxed by the amount of time we are giving ourselves.

I post my three month goal calendars above my workspace and look at them often. The lists resonate within me more and more each time I see my goals and speak them out loud, they become real to me and I become motivated. Try not to put your goals in a place where you cannot consistently see them. Ever heard of, "Out of sight, out of mind?"

When writing down your goals, be detailed and specific. Do not just write, "Monetize from my blog." Dig deeper. How will you monetize from your blog? How much do you hope to monetize per month? What is your timeline of when you hope to see your first check?

Getting this detailed on your "Monetize from my blog" goal will give yourself a better understanding of what direction you are wanting to take and need to take to get to the ultimate goal. This will help you create your breakdown of smaller goals to get to your ultimate goal.

Next you will want to put a timeline next to all of your goals, small or big. Some may only take a week to complete, some a month, and some 3 months to complete. Whatever it is, write down the timeline. It will increase your eagerness to get the tasks done.

Example:

Pinterest Follower Goals: 1,000 within first 3 months of blogging
  • Find a free webinar about Pinterest presence by end of month to learn how to grow a following.
  • By end of month two, have Pinterest follow me links up on site,
  • Include Pinterest links in subscribers emails.
  • Pin 60 times a day on Pinterest to set a presence.
  • Get on 5 group boards by end of month three.

In the beginning learning all the technical parts of the working a blog took a lot of time for me, so having longer deadlines on installing links, plugins, and such was ok for me. I was learning and I wanted to make sure I was choosing the best plugins and links for my site. The majority of my time went into reading reviews and researching. I no longer have this barrier, now this is something that has become simpler to me through experience.

Do not pressure yourself too much on where you should be at and the time in which it should be done. Be realistic to yourself and if you get done sooner then great, you are a step closer in a shorter time. Mission accomplished!

I highly recommend to also set goals in other areas of your life. This goal list can be completely separate in a personal letter or goal setting format to yourself. In blogging you can get distracted by many tasks that are needed as you grow your blog which means you can easily lose focus of your loved ones, your full time job, parenting, schooling, church, and just about anything in your personal life. Write down areas that you do not want to get consumed by and what you hope to achieve to make sure that blogging does not overwhelm you. By writing this down, it will help you subconsciously to make sure you are keeping to it.

I usually do not do as well as I want but I do work on it and get better at it each day. I set boundaries for myself of when and how long to be on social media, writing, editing, and all that involves with blogging.

As you will read in the next chapter "Creating Space," my most successful ways I work and achieve my daily "to do list" is by time blocking. This is probably one of the most recommended ways to work. Time Blocking is setting a schedule in increments. One hour of complete concentration in the morning, 30 minutes in the afternoon, and 1 hour at night. These increments work best for specific projects or duties that are part of your blog, not necessarily for the entire work of the blog per day.

As I started working on my book, this plan worked best for me because I knew those slotted times were only for writing the book, nothing about the blog. For the blog, I work 4 hours in the day and roughly two hours at night. To make best of my time, I make 30 minute increments. The first 30 minutes are for emails and comments. The next 30 minutes are for social media, followed by an hour of writing new content, and so on....

One thing I do every first day of the month is pull out my tracker sheet. Keeping track of my blogging progress has been my biggest encouragement to sticking to my plan and timeline for set goals. When I see an increase of progress, I get excited that my plans and goals have met the challenge. When I see a decrease, I check where I lacked and I work on improvement. It drives a determination in me.

Some goals we will not be able to track. As a Christian blogger our purpose is to do God's will first; God's will and direction in our lives is not to be merited. Scripture even speaks about the one soul. God doesn't look at accounting He looks for a witness in the kingdom. There is no metric system of goals in ministry but there is contentment and peace. There is great achievement in being a blogger that does not struggle with envy or comparison of whose goals got them higher or more.

Takeaway Tip: Purchase a Planner. One that you will be able to write notes in and that has time tables so you can write your tasks per hour. Begin creating a schedule. Your schedule with blogging will generally change monthly due to your blog growing, more tasks and the greater the tasks the more time consuming it will be. So I suggest monthly planning, unless you have a deadline to meet then you can write anywhere on the planner that is needed.

− 5 −

Create Space

When I first started blogging, my plan was to work throughout the day as I had time. As my two youngest played and crawled around I would sit on the floor with my laptop and type away. My ears were perked and eyes were ready to follow my babies. This worked for me for a few months.

I felt I was doing the right thing by working with my children's schedule; by working with them in front of me, but it suddenly all caught up with me.

Over time my seat down on the floor became uncomfortable and my children's need for undivided attention increased. So my attention span for the blog began to decline while the tasks for the blog were increasingly growing.

At the end of month three, I went around my home looking for pieces to pull together to create a work space. I found an old desk of mine in the spare bedroom, plenty of inspirational framed art and a bookcase of prayer filled books to begin designing my area that would now be designated only for blogging.

An area just for your blogging keeps you focused. You are able to sit down in your seat with purpose and a mindset of developing new ideas.

As a stay at home mom, I still needed to work around my children's schedule but sitting on the floor with them was not how

I was supposed to continue working on the blog any longer.

I kept hearing a voice tell me within my spirit that I could not blog about spending undivided time with my children but yet I was having my children starve for undivided attention right in front of my eyes.

I felt the Holy Spirit tell me what I am writing is the life I am living not what I am trying to live or what I want people to think I am living. I want to be an example to my children and readers alike. When I created my space, I sat down and rewrote my new normal day, the new look of Monday through Friday. I included which days I usually went grocery shopping, times of naps, times we woke up and went to bed, days I had sporting or school events. I did my best to write down every detail of my family's day. I then began to fill in time slots of where I could write and blog without it interrupting my family's life.

Waking up an extra hour or two would have been well allowed. Two hours in the afternoon during naptime met my day time need of sending a presence of myself in social medias. Working at night after my family was in bed, was and is a great fit for me. I am much more of a night person and feel more productive working at night than I do in the morning. Weekends are and will always be optional for me to work.

As your blog grows, so do the tasks. Some days may seem like an hour here or two hours there is not enough. Most days it will not be enough; this is where it will take a lot of practice in time management and prioritizing to become effective and efficient at utilizing your time.

Along with using a planner and goal sheets to make sure I am staying on track of what is important to me, I began to time block my tasks. This has been successful for me. This practice keeps me focused and consistent.

Time blocking is setting a determined time ahead that focuses on your priorities. For example if you begin working at 7am and you are committing 2 hours to working on the blog without any interruptions then you can itemize your time based by priority. First 15 minutes for checking emails. The next 30 minutes on social media, responding to comments, engaging with other bloggers and interacting with followers, and 1 hour to writing content. Lastly, go through your to do list for that day.

Here is an example of my time blocks throughout the day Monday through Friday. Each day is the same except for two days out of the week because those are the days I post new postings to the blog and will require more and different tasks.

Two hours in the morning

7:00 am - 7:30 am Prayer and Bible Study
7:30 am - 7:45 am Pin and/or Schedule Pins if needed
7:45 am - 8:30 am Check emails, blog comments, social media comments, engagement with others on social media.
8:30 am - 9:00 am Work on content. Write.

Two hours in the afternoon

12:00 pm - 12:30 pm Create images for new content.
12:30 pm - 2:00 pm Write content and post new content.

Two hours in the evening

9:00 pm - 9:30 pm Check emails, social media and blog comments.
9:30 pm - 10:15 pm Read others blog posts, leave a positive comment, pin or post on social media.
10:15 pm - 10:30 pm Complete any tasks from the day.
10:30 pm - 11:00 pm Write.

If you would like to take this a step further as I have, you can detail your tasks. See the examples below for when I am working on my social media. Sticking to my suggested tasks keeps my focus and keeps me within my time boundaries.

Example - Social media:

Instagram: Like 5 pics, comment on others. Post 1-2 times a day.

Twitter: Like 5 tweets, retweet one other blogger post, tweet a favorite blog post from someone else, tweet one of my own post.

Facebook: Post content in groups for designated days, engage with others in groups.

This is not always the exact schedule for my social medias but this does give me a great foundation to work with. It reminds me of how important my social media presence is for the blog and for the blogger community.

The tip to being focused and having time blocking be successful for you is to not have any windows on your desktop open or having any other distractions like a cell phone or any social medias accessible to you.

Once a timed task has elapsed then switch immediately to the next task and so on and so on.

It takes practice but by working with my time block I have become so free from fumbling over what was next to do on the blog. Time blocking has also helped me tremendously with my accountability to the blog.

When you create a space and a plan, you are also creating a stress free zone. This is needed for any blogger or work from home person.

Takeaway Tip: Create a Time Block Schedule. Create one for each day you plan to work. Choose two to three days you would like to post new content for the blog. Be specific and detailed on what your tasks will be for each day. Print out your Time Block Schedule and post it in your work space. Keep the schedule at eye level where you can continuously see it while in your work area.

– 6 –

Cultivating Your Blog into a Ministry

Cultivating your blog into a ministry is a daily act and choice. The dictionary defines *cultivate* as this: To promote or improve growth by labor and attention; to devote one's self (to growth and maturity).

Cultivating takes time, pruning, and attention to detail. It requires pulling up the weeds that are choking your blogging ministry. It requires fresh water to nourish and a good eye to see where it is becoming lifeless.

I believe the above scenario can relate to our blogs. It is up to us to keep our ministry full of life and thriving. Our care, attention to detail, and devotion keeps our blog and ministry enriched. The Lord has entrusted us with this ministry so it is our responsibility to tend to all the needs of the the blog that will allow it to prosper.

Consistent maintenance to your blog will be vital to building a ministry from it. Being active on your blog will continue to bring life to many souls that are seeking maturity and growth from the word of God. As you cultivate your blog keep in mind that this is done by the leading of God and the willingness to be a humble vessel.

It has been a honor to watch Married by His Grace blog grow into a ministry but just as I mentioned above, it is a lot of work.

Cultivating my blog into a ministry is a daily choice I have to make every day and so is being connected with the Lord for the well-being of myself and the ministry I am growing. Ultimately, my perseverance and dedication to the maturity of the blog is also factored into my own continuous growth and maturity in Christ.

Cultivating your blog into a ministry is being in a place of obedience for the Lord. This is where you want to be when you are creating, building, and maintaining a ministry because this is not about our desires any longer but knowing that this is all because of what the Lord is requiring for us to do. This does not mean we are no longer to be ourselves it means that we are growing into what we were created to be.

I have continuously been reminded by the Lord, 'Created for a Purpose on Purpose'. What I depend on each day and desire to have materialistically is all for but a moment. However, His purpose on my life is all for eternity. Understanding this keeps me from being stagnant of cultivation because the awareness of His purpose keeps me diligent to the work He has entrusted to me do.

> *"Therefore, brothers, be all the more diligent to make your calling and election sure, for if you practice these qualities you will never fall. For in this way there will be richly provided for you an entrance into the eternal kingdom of our Lord and Savior Jesus Christ."*   *2 Peter 10-11 ESV*

Since the beginning of my blogging journey, I knew within the depths of me that I would not write about anything but of Him. As I began the journey I saw that the blog was cultivating, it was creating a ministry that was growing and flourishing. Not by my will but by His will and leading.

Honestly at the beginning this scared me. The thoughts of who am I to do this feared me to point of not wanting to write any longer. The thought of accountability overwhelmed me. And I knew by developing and maintaining the cultivation of my blog, my accountability was going to increase and the thought left me feeling defeated.

I thought about all the times I allowed my flesh to take over and may have said hurtful words to my husband when I really didn't mean to or how I had just gotten upset at my two year old for coloring on the table and how I was not a gracefully responding mother. The thoughts of, how can I write about being a graceful mother if I can not handle the sight of a blue and green colored table top? Will the readers still want to read from someone like me? Will they see through me and think my words about marriage are no longer reliable if they found out that I was upset at my husband last weekend for not taking out the trash once again?

I allowed myself to believe that creating a blog for His purpose was supposed to be me representing perfection. But this was not God telling me this. His will for the blog was for me to speak truth and grace with obedience even with my flaws because truth is given through conviction, grace is understood by experience, and obedience is done by willingness. These were the moments God wanted me to learn, understand, and then write to women who felt the same way, are experiencing the same things, and bearing through the same as me. To give them a perspective of what He is able to do.

The word tells us:

> "For we do not wrestle against flesh and blood, but against the rulers, against the authorities, against the cosmic powers over this present darkness, against the spiritual forces of evil in the heavenly places."   Ephesians 6:12 ESV

Because of the fear, my blog began to become stagnant. to begin recultivating the blog, I had to come to a place of peace of mind and contentment with what God was doing so I began to seek insight in this area.

One day I came across a fellow blogger's blog and read, "Don't be afraid to grow your blog for the glory of God." This one statement became powerful to me personally because I faced fear in this area for quite a while. But for some reason when I read this specific statement boldness suddenly grew within me. It gave me the confidence I needed to overcome my own fears of failure.

As the quote sunk in, the soil of the cultivation began to turn to rich soil. The look of the blog began to look fresh and glowing once again through my eyes. It no longer looked tired and withered. Before I knew it the blog grew into something not of my own abilities or inabilities, but it was from the freedom of the fear and from the leading of God.

See yourself as someone that is cultivating a ministry, vision a crop, not just a plant. Every person that reads the words the Lord has given you is part of the cultivation. His words expand and grow beyond our measurement. Vision the land enlarging as you maintain it. Do not fear the outcome but instead embrace the growth with the same faith that you have built the crops with.

> *The Lord answered, "If you had faith even as small as a mustard seed, you could say to this mulberry tree, 'May you be uprooted and thrown into the sea,' and it would obey you!*
> *Luke 17:6 NLT*

Takeaway Tip: Create a mission statement. The mission statement should have one to two sentences that are concise and to the point of what your blog's name is, who is the blog for (demographic), and what does it provide (its purpose). The mission statement should also have one sentence of the vision and future of your blog. By doing this, you are building your measure of faith and enlarging your land of crops through your ministry.

− 7 −
Blog to Business

Is your dream to become a business owner through your blog? Do you want to eventually monetize from your blog? Do you hope to make an income, part time or full time from your blog?

If so, then treating your blog as a business from the very beginning will be a beneficial action you can take to create a monetizing blog.

Whether you are about to start a blog or you are an experienced blogger, if you decide to monetize your blog then from this day forward it is time to treat your blog like you are in business.

Before becoming successful with your blog, it is important for you to have a realization that a blog is not an overnight sensation that immediately delivers payday after payday. A blog that is your business should not be consumed by the factor of income.

Turning your blog into a business is exciting but the purpose of your blog can not be just to make money, it needs to be greater than that as a focus. The passion cannot run out otherwise you will be burned out and the business will not succeed.

You need to be the number one believer in what you are writing and selling which means your passion for your writing content and products you hope to offer has to exceed the desire of monetizing from a business itself.

A blogger whose focus is only on growing and prospering into a small business usually fails early on by the spirit of envy and comparison.

Do not fall into the place of comparing one blog business to the next. This right here is already claiming failure. Once you begin to compare you are no longer into your successes but other successes that you cannot control. By comparing you will be on a constant wheel going in circles. It leads to nowhere but feeling dizzy and lost.

As you noticed, I used the word spirit when describing envy and comparison because as a Christian blogger I believe it is important to know that you are capable of changing this type of mindset. You are greater than the darts that are being flung at you. I often tell myself 'Mind over Matter'. Even I, as a believer in Christ, have to have full confidence that the matter of the situation cannot take over my mind, which is what Christ bought a price with for us.

I am someone that battles the darts of "Who am I to do this?" Who am I to blog to thousands that look at my blog each month?" Who am I to write this book to encourage a fellow blogger?" But the Lord reminds me, "You are who I, the Lord chose to do my works, not your own." As a women that has reverence for the Lord, it convicts me and brings me back to His instruction to conquer the thoughts and seek the courage I need to write words, build a community, and enhance my knowledge in all that I do for the will of God.

I would like you to step back to what you learned in chapter one before stepping forward to the next few chapters about monetizing your blog. Before blogging becomes profitable for you, is this the will of God for your blog? Was this the original plan the Lord spoke to you or even spoke to you after already investing time into your blog? For some, the requests are known to them step by step, some may not know the plan of monetizing was there for them till they complete one task wholeheartedly from the Lord till the next. The Lord can open doors at any time after seeing you complete one task He requested of you. For example, He may request; simply blog to spread the gospel or simply blog to encourage your fellow blogging community.

Before deciding to monetize from your blog or brand I want you to deeply and intimately seek God about this. This may be the simple act the Lord needs from you before taking the hand of your labor to the next level.

I do believe God has set some blogging entrepreneurs from the workplace to full time blogging to do His will and be able to earn an income from it so they can do His work full time. But if you are trying to do this before His timing, much discouragement may follow just as much as if we try to do anything else outside of blogging out of His will.

Majority of bloggers still work full time but would like to eventually have blogging as their full time income, so let's talk about this next.

If you are in the position that you need to work full time as you start your entrepreneurial talents on blogging, then becoming an expert in time management will need to become a second language to you. Blogging can become overwhelming and tiring especially if you are just trying to hurry and build an empire overnight, which by the way I need to tell you is not realistic. Even the most successful bloggers (audience and monetary) did not make it overnight. As a blogger you are most likely solo. You are the marketing director, the writer, the web designer, the technology team, and the only person on the team to encourage you to keep going.

Blogging will take time to build as a business that can lead you to quit your full time job. There are many many testimonies out there of bloggers being able to do this, but till God has called you out of the workplace and given you the provision and tools that you will need to achieve the needs of the home, do not jeopardize your full time income because of the blog.

This is not a matter of faith that you have in yourself or your blog, it is a matter of wisdom by allowing God to be the leader over your home, finances, and plans. As a married wife, wisdom is also standing in agreement with our spouse before making any decisions.

As we now go forward and go more in depth of treating your blog as a business, the best piece of advice I can give you is: keep yourself motivated to learn daily about building a business, marketing, financial wisdom, and creating content. Learning every day for the sake of your blog is what will keep you motivated and knowledgeable to do great things for the blog.

There are a few details that will make your blog look like a personal blog versus a blog of an entrepreneur and leader in your niche. Here are a few steps to take as someone that would like to create that look for their own business:

- Create a mission statement.
- Prepare yourself with a business plan
- Begin planning. Calendar yourself for yearly, quarterly, monthly, and daily goals.
- Be specific and decisive as you develop a brand. Stick to the brand you choose.
- Learn what marketing is and treat it as a vital part of your blog.
- Be consistent. Choose a schedule of when to post and do your best to stick to the days.
- Find a mentor that you trust and believes in you and your vision. Who will give you godly wisdom as you build a blog that is for the purpose of God's will.

When you do the following for your blog, you are enriching yourself with a head start of a well prosperous blog which will then lead you to where God wants to grow your blog.

Takeaway Tip: Purchase a Planner. One that you will be able to write notes in and that has time tables so you can write your tasks per hour. Begin creating a schedule. Your schedule with blogging will generally change monthly due to your blog growing, more tasks and the greater the tasks will become more time consuming so I suggest planning by per month, unless you have a deadline then you can write anywhere on the planner that is needed.

– 8 –

Creating a Brand

Branding as a blogger is not defined by just the logo you choose but it describes what your purpose and vision is to your audience.

The process is not only determined by the same physical appearance across the board, branding is what you desire for your audience to receive you and your product as. The setting and tone of your brand is what will draw your audience in.

I love how *businessdictionary.com* puts the definition of branding:

"The process involved in creating a unique name and image for a product in the consumer's' mind, mainly through advertising campaigns with a consistent theme. Branding aims to establish a significant and differentiated presence in the market that attracts and retains loyal customers."

What is your differentiated presence in the market? What are you offering to your readers that no one else is? How do you show that?

For me, the most important thing that I want to show how different I am from the millions of others bloggers is that I am a Christian writer. My blog first represents Christ. This right away puts me into a smaller category which is a valuable move for me and my brand. Because instead of being in front of a lot of people who do not have the same interests as me, I am now in front of people that have the same interests.

When gaining your targeted audience you will want to do as read in the definition of creating a brand; 'making a trademark is creating a consistent look'. When creating a brand you must make sure it is the same all across the board.

Consistency in blogging is also a key factor to branding. Profile Picture, profile bio, color schemes, fonts, and personality traits (your audience will expect the same tone of personality from you). Be consistent when you post new blog content and when you post in social media.

Your profile picture in every social media or platform that has your website attached to your blog should have the same profile picture. Reason for this is to make sure you are recognizable. You do not want a reader to wonder if they finally found you on social media or not. You want them to see your picture and know immediately they found you. Not everyone will take the time to search for you even though for the past 15 minutes they just read your blog. This is a fast paced world that people are used to having social media as a simplicity outlet so being consistent in your look is important to this very reason

You will want to portray an overall consistency of your personality and blog. What are you expecting your readers to expect from you and your writings? A silly or formal person? Sentimental or encouraging writer? A conservative or informal bio picture. There is no right or wrong answer. It just about authentically being you. You want to show them who God created you to be and what He chose for you to be used for. Which means you must be honest about who you are in Christ.

If you do not know who this is yet. Seek God about it. Do not be ashamed of this and think any less of yourself. I had to seek God. I wasn't sure who I desired for my readers to see me as. A wife that loves to serve my husband, a mothers that has an spiritually authoritative voice for my children, or a women that is trying to fulfill these roles. I wondered about all those areas till the Lord showed me to be all of them because that is who I am. I am not one or the other, I am all of them. I shouldn't try to be like the other blogger that I think has it all together.

The best way to express your personality and what your blog is about is through your profiles on all the social medias or any other platforms you use for your blog. Make sure you mention your love for Christ so that whoever follows you knows what to expect from you and your blog. As a Christian blogger it's important to add your relationship with God within those few sentences because it will develop the loyal readers you want. They will know what to expect from you and your blog. When they follow you, it will be because they have the same faith as you and are like minded as you which will develop a relationship between you and them.

With my bio picture being the same on each social media platform I use you can also see that all my profile bios are close to the same.

Instagram: Christian Blogger | Wife | Mother | Encouraging women to build a Christ like home. Passionate about teaching New Christian Bloggers. Check out Blog:

Pinterest: Christian Blogger encouraging women to build their homes with Christ! Passionate about teaching New Christian Bloggers to start a blog. Check out blog for tips!

Twitter: Encouraging woman to build a Christ like home with His mercy and grace. Passionate about teaching new Christian Bloggers.

Facebook: I am chasing after God while encouraging women to build a Christ like home with His Mercy and Grace.

Depending on the the length of words you are able to use, each one will differ but as you can see, they do not need to defer by much. Use different wording to shorten sentences in some areas if you are running out of space.

Social media presence is important to your brand because it speaks volumes to your readers. Do you engage? Are you consistent? Are your platforms clean or messy?

My Instagram may not be the picture perfect feed but my blog references are consistent and my personal pics show who I am. I am a mother and wife that loves my cozy home and shares my happy moments. The moments that God touches my heart with.

Branding is exposing your personality and the demeanor of your blog and products. How you expose yourself will determine your following; do not see this as a downfall. In the contrary this is a good thing, the ones that chooses to follow you will be because they fell in love with you, with who you are and they like your personality which will make them into loyal readers. I rather have a small group of loyal readers then a mass group that does not know me.

As a beginner blogger, do not pressure yourself into having a well-known brand overnight, as long as you are being consistent your brand will evolve as your blog grows.

Besides the topical part of branding with things such as selecting: a color scheme, two favorite fonts to consistently use, a profile picture that will be used throughout social media and blog, you should also be thinking about what you post. I know this is digging a little deeper but it is important and must be discussed in the topic of branding.

Everything you post is representing who you are and what you are blogging about. Sounds a little dramatic, huh?! I am not trying to be dramatic, I am just being honest. Everything you post on social media is representing you and the blog which is hopefully all in all representing Christ first.

I once read a post about branding and it expressed the importance of what you post is who you are and even brands that you hope to work with one day will notice that too. If you are or hope to monetize one day from your blog, I hope you find this info valuable and a good insight to keep in mind. Potential partners that you can eventually work with will want to know they can trust you and your judgement.

However, if you are following Christ and doing His will for your blog then what you post should not be a concern. You are a leader as a blogger of your own site. As a leader you are sending out words to encourage, uplift, and to fulfill a ministry. Bear fruit of hope, righteousness, kindness, and self-control with it.

This is how one should regard us, as servants of Christ and stewards of the mysteries of God. Moreover, it is required of stewards that they be found trustworthy.
1 Corinthians 4:1-2

Takeaway Tip: I hope you take time to check over all your social medias that has your blog attached to it and check if you have the same picture and similar profile. I know each social media gives you so many characters and you will not be able to create identical profiles to each social media but you can make them similar.

— 9 —

Understanding Pinterest

Before using Pinterest I think it's important to understand the platform and get a good perception of how important Pinterest truly is to a blogger.

As a blogger one thing that breaks my heart the most is when I see other bloggers not using Pinterest. It is literally a game changer and needs to be thought of as a planned action to build your blog.

Here are a few statistics about Pinterest that will give you a better understanding of how well the dynamic platform can work for you as a blogger.

- Close to 70% of Pinterest users are women and 50% of them have children.
- Most common age is between 25-34 years old.
- Increasingly rising, over 30% of online active users are starting to choose Pinterest over Google as a search engine. Being mostly used as a bookmarking tool for future plans and inspiration
- Pinterest has a consistent 111% active member growth each month and is known to be as the fastest growing platform with active members.
- More than 80% of Pins are Repins which means a pinned post has a higher chance of going viral, especially since average time for a Pin to last on Pinterest is months, not

hours or days, like Facebook or Twitter.

- 58% Pinterest users purchase products from Pins they have pinned.
- 80% of Pinterest users will click on products that is shown with a price of the product on the image which leads to a higher purchase rate than any other social media platform.

Now that you know some statistics, here is a list of how using Pinterest will bring growth to your blog.

- Your blog will be in front of thousands active users
- Higher chances for your blog to be noticed by influencers in your niche/industry
- Increases your chances for viral pins
- You will be able to reach your targeted audience to your blog
- You will receive more subscribers to your blog as your traffic from Pinterest increases.

Ways to use Pinterest for you blog:

- Ability to pin vlogs and videos
- Able to tell your brand's story with your Pinterest boards and pins
- Display your products
- Able to pin affiliate marketing and your own product.
- Inspiration
- Highest rate of active users
- Best visual tool
- Shoppers referred from Pinterest are most likely to buy

Now, if this does not convince you that Pinterest is a must for a blogger then I do not know what will. I hope to have showed you there is unlimited potential for your blog to grow in the free platform.

Takeaway Tip: If you have not yet done so, get yourself familiar with using Pinterest. Research for Pinterest Tips as a blogger and find Pinterest Webinars (preferably free, there are many out there once you start the search). Becoming comfortable with Pinterest will take away the what ifs and questions to is this really worth your blog's time which is the number one barrier to most bloggers out there that is not using Pinterest.

– 10 –

How to Use Pinterest

This chapter will be packed with information on how to use Pinterest. There is a substantial amount of knowledge to learn about Pinterest. Two important things you should know about Pinterest as a blogger is that it brings in the highest amount of traffic for active bloggers and it is the best free marketing tool for online entrepreneurs.

As a blogger that is currently receiving over 90% of my monthly page views from Pinterest, this is unreal and a blessing rolled up into a beautiful strategic plan, if used correctly! There is a strategy to using Pinterest and if you want to use Pinterest as a free marketing tool than it is necessary for you to put the work it into.

I had a Pinterest account for nearly two years with sixty followers. The day I started blogging I took the Pinterest game pretty serious by researching and attending webinars specifically about Pinterest and marketing a blog.

By the end of my first three months of blogging and implementing what I have learned from other bloggers that were willing to share their tips, I was up 500% growth in followers and 1200% page views because of visits from Pinterest.

The strategy begins from the beginning step; starting a Pinterest account. I will be sharing step by step of how to start a Pinterest account as a blogger and how to use the platform for your blogs benefit.

Create a Pinterest Business Account:

When creating an account as a blogger you will want to open a Pinterest Business Account which you can do when you open a new account. If you already have a personal Pinterest account you can convert to a business. All you will need is your website domain name to do this. Once you complete the registration and you are set up as a business account you will verify the account through your Settings page. In Settings you will click confirm which is next to the website field and follow the remaining instructions. By confirming your website; your domain name will appear on your pins and will show potential followers that your website was confirmed through Pinterest as an active site. Verification will assure potential followers and readers you are a trusted website.

Profile Bio:

You Pinterest bio will be your first impression. This is your chance to show potential followers and readers what you and your blog are all about. My recommendation is to choose four to five verbs that describes you and your blog. With those verbs create three to four sentences that will characterize you and your blog. For the last sentence in your profile create it to be a lead magnet. Why should they visit your blog? Do you have a freebie, sign up bonus, training tutorials or webinars? What is it that they can learn and gain from you? If you have one, this should be in the last sentence. A good profile will also consist of a profile picture of yourself, it should be bright, vibrant, and professional.

Creating your Pinterest Boards:

Creating a cohesive look is a significant part of creating a brand. Pinterest is part of your brand so when you are creating a Pinterest account you should keep this in mind. You will also want the color schemes of your boards to look similiar to your blogs and social media platforms. Keeping a consistent look to your boards will also help when a potential follower looks at your account. They will look to see what you have to offer from your boards. Looking cohesive will make it simple for them to do that.

If the boards you had before becoming a blogger does not have a cohesive look but you do not want to delete your pins or previous boards then you can change the board covers by clicking onto your board. You will then click Edit which looks like a pencil emblem; this will be placed above your board's title. Change the board cover in the pop up box. You will be able to change your cover to any of the pins you had already pinned onto that specific board. Do this to all your active boards till you get the look you want. Choose a pin that will achieve the color scheme you desire.

Besides group boards; ideally you should have 25-30 boards on your Pinterest Profile. They should all be titled of a topic that is within your blog's niche. When you do this, it will let your followers know what to consistently expect from you. For example if your Blog is about Christian Marriage, your boards could be of: Marriage, Family, Parenting, Ministry, Following God, Scriptures.

Make sure to use keywords. Pinterest is a search engine for images. When you use keywords for your boards or blog posts you will have a greater chance to be seen.

The first board in your profile should always be of your blog posts. Most bloggers like to title it "The best of (blogs name)." I personally just title the board of my blog's name: 'Married by His Grace.'

Establish your presence:

This step is an important one before you can get to the step of joining Pinterest group boards. This step is about 'Time'. Time is what you need to have your presence on Pinterest established and to be able to have more of a free reign in the area of joining group boards. Although I love inviting and receiving requests for new bloggers onto my Pinterest group boards, not everyone feels the same. Some boards I couldn't join or even receive responses about joining for months.

The waiting months accumulated to more followers, more boards, and more repins. Any reliable group board creator will want their boards to succeed and sometimes this means only accepting invites from those that are steadily growing with their own boards.

Establish yourself by consistently pinning each day. Give yourself a goal of how many pins a day you would like to do. Some bloggers strive to pin 30 a day and others strive for a 100 pins a day. 100 is a very hard reach but can be done. And although you can do it, I do not recommend it because the amount of time this task consumes.

I do not recommend to continue any blogging task that can cause a issue in other areas in your life. Besides from my own content my goal is to pin 40 a day. I pin about 10-15 pins once in the morning, 10-15 in the afternoon, then again in the evening.

Joining Group Boards:

Joining Group Boards is one of the most valuable things you can do to gain a following on Pinterest and to get traffic to your blog. Besides Group Boards being known to put your blog's name in a large audience, Group boards also gets you and your blog noticed by influencers in your niche.

As active Pinterest members see your pinned post, they will also see your Pinterest profile picture on the Pin which will let them see the human side of you; which will let you see the anointed writer that you hope for them to see.

Depending on the group boards you join, you can possibly be getting in front of thousands of other pinners within seconds from pinning your posts to the group board which eventually can lead to higher amount of traffic to your blog and increase your chances of having a post go viral.

The important factor about joining groups is to join groups that is within your niche. Joining group boards with like-minded people helps you get to your target audience. You do not want to join a group board that is specifically being catered to Fitness Bloggers just because you were accepted on a board but yet you are a Bible Study Blogger. Do not take this to be flattering. It is
not flattering to not get the targeted audience you need. If those followers are deliberately following the group board because of the Fitness Pins that it contains then the chance of them clicking on your link is low.

One of the best ways I have found group boards to join is to look at boards of bloggers that I follow in that same niche as myself. Any boards that have the people icon on the right hand corner is a group board. I would click on the board they were participating on and read the profile bio. If I liked what the group board was representing, I would follow the instructions of how to join. Not all creators post how to join so I will personally message the creator of the board with a polite note requesting an invite to join their group board.

If you send a personal message please use the etiquette of adding your name and your website link so they may visit if they choose to. Also include the link to your Pinterest account so they can add you easily.

A simple "Hello, Can I join your group board?" leaves the receiver lost of how to find you and not knowing what your blog represents. By doing this, they cannot discern if you line up with their guidelines or requirements.

Creating Pin Worthy Images

Good images are the backbone to Pinterest. Pinterest was created for the visuals, so immediately grabbing your potential readers' attention with the image and title is a vital part to the Pinterest strategy.

As of now I use Pexels.com and Canva.com and here's why; it's free! Majority of the images are also free. You can purchase stock images from the sites but you do not need to, there is plenty to choose from without having to spend a penny.

Five simple tips on how to create Pin worthy images:

1. Image should be vertical.
2. Best size to use on Pinterest is: 700px x 1100px or 800px x 1200px
3. Your Blog's name should always be on the image. Keep it consistent by using the same font and placement of your Blog's name each time.
4. Choose a color scheme. Images are not always going to be cohesive but if you choose a color scheme you like then you will be mindful to be cohesive. Some bloggers choose a signature color for their blog's title.
5. Creating a title to put on the image that will grab attention is important. The title is what will pull a reader in after you grabbed their attention with the image. Titles should be about what they will get out of the post. What will they learn or gain from it. Top titles for blog posts begin with:

"5 ways you can......"
" How I .... and you can too!"

"The Ultimate guide to....."
"How to ....."

People want to learn new things and want to hear how you did it before they do it that is why these titles do so well.

For a Christian Blogger that generally writes about the Word of God and our own testimonies this may seem a little unrelated but it really isn't. Here are some examples of how you can use the top titles for blog posts for your blog:

"How God took me through....."
"How I learned to become graceful through ...."
"How I was revived....."
"The Ultimate Guide to Marriage Resources....."

Be creative with your titles. Although this is an area that I feel I lack creativity in, this is still one of my favorite things to work on after creating my image. I feel like the title completes the post and the look of the image.

Takeaway Tip: Start a Pinterest Business Account. Create your blog's board on your Profile then create 25-30 more to have on your profile. Try to keep the board's topic the same as your niche.

– 11 –

Monetizing from a Christian Blog

If you are struggling with the thoughts about making money from your blog, it could be a good thing. That is a good struggle to have. This means you are being cautious and desire to take heed to God's leading instead of where monetizing can lead.

It is very rare that you will see Christian Bloggers post anything about income reports or if they even make an income. This is probably because receiving money for what we feel is a ministry for the Lord is a sensitive topic for most. Although I believe in being conservative in the matter of money and how much we should share with one another, I think there is a need among the group of Christian Bloggers to conversate about this topic.

I know I started blogging because the Lord led me to blog but I also knew from the very beginning it could become a source of income. Do not complicate that statement with the thought that my motivation of blogging was to earn a source of income because that is not the case.

I did not know how or when. As far as I knew it would take years or it would just be enough to keep my blog going and that was something that I was already content with if that was the result.

Even knowing all of this, I still questioned if monetizing as a

Christian Blogger was ok for me to do. Is it spiritually moral? Would God really allow me to earn an income through writing His words?

When I first started a blog those questions about monetizing from a blog that ministers to women with the word of God; overwhelmed me. I felt like it was wrong on some levels. I would often kneel in prayer to the Lord about this specific situation. I wanted God Himself to come down and confirm to me that it was not illegitimate to make money from blogging that was about Him and that my concerns of earning an income were settled by Him.

I believed I struggled with this because I was not yet confident in the vision God was giving me. I did not see how He was strategically leading me into a place of contentment. I was more worried about what others were thinking, that I missed what God was saying.

It finally hit me one day like rocks trembling down from the big mountain I was trying to move with my little faith. The revelation was of simple words; "God is ok with this."

How I finally got to the revelation was because during this questionable time about monetizing I emailed my dearest blogging friend that I knew I would only receive godly counsel from. I asked her what she thought about monetizing with our fairly new blogs. She replied with this question, "Would you still blog about His word if you did make an income then it one day stopped?" The challenge of this question was to see the bigger picture of why we blog.

Her email then continued with asking me to read the below scriptures:

"For it is written in the Law of Moses, "YOU SHALL NOT MUZZLE THE OX WHILE HE IS THRESHING." God is not concerned about

oxen, is He? Or is He speaking altogether for our sake? Yes, for our sake it was written, because the plowman ought to plow in hope, and the thresher to thresh in hope of sharing the crops. If we sowed spiritual things in you, is it too much if we reap material things from you? If others share the right over you, do we not more? Nevertheless, we did not use this right, but we endure all things so that we will cause no hindrance to the gospel of Christ. Do you not know that those who perform sacred services eat the food of the temple, and those who attend regularly to the altar have their share from the altar? So also the Lord directed those who proclaim the gospel to get their living from the gospel. But I have used none of these things. And I am not writing these things so that it will be done so in my case; for it would be better for me to die than have any man make my boast an empty one. For if I preach the gospel, I have nothing to boast of, for I am under compulsion; for woe is me if I do not preach the gospel."

1 Corinthians 9:9-16 NASB

She then encouraged me by stating there are many anointed Christian Bloggers making an income with their God given talent and we should not be afraid to be able to do the same if God called us. We just have to make sure to not have the money to be the motivator of creating a blog. We need to be in a place of contentment even if we never do make an income because the truth is, this is all for the glory of God.

Before ending the email she did one last thing that I would expect from any trusting sister in Christ, she reminded me to pay my tithes and offering if I was to ever earn.

Her humbling response left me speechless. The rain of revelation came pouring down. I heard myself say "If I am doing His will then my thoughts would not be on man but by His leading and direction for the blog. God is ok with this."

As we read from the scripture, monetizing from spreading the gospel is ok and allowed. Paul spoke this to ensure that the ones that are doing this are paid, fed, clothed, and well taken care of. Paul did not say this for himself but for the well-being of others. Monetizing may not be for you just as it was not for Paul but because Paul did not receive does not mean it was not allowed. It just meant that you have to connect with the Lord on this matter and know if this is where the Lord is leading you and your blog.

My personal hope is for all of us to earn an income through Christian Blogging so that we can enjoy doing our ministry from home, with our families and with no financial doubts, but this is selfish of me because this is not everyone's purpose.
Maybe the richness of some Christian Bloggers is learning the concept of obedience or gaining the spiritual growth that they have been desiring. Some have been called to preach the gospel without financial concerns and to stand up with truth and grace just as Paul did. Every situation is different and unique and all though we hope these things for others, those hopes are no greater than God's hope and plans for us.

His word tells us,

> 'For I know the plans that I have for you,' declares the LORD, 'plans for welfare and not for calamity to give you a future and a hope.'
>
> *Jeremiah 29:11 NASB*

As we continue to read we will see that in seeking God through prayer He will provide the fortunes that He planned for us to have:

> Then you will call upon Me and come and pray to Me, and I will listen to you. You will seek Me and find Me when you search for Me with all your heart. I will be found by you,' declares the LORD, 'and I will restore your fortunes and will gather

you from all the nations and from all the places where I have driven you,' declares the LORD, 'and I will bring you back to the place from where I sent you into exile.'

Jeremiah 29: 12-14 NASB

He is driving us from nation to nation to spread the gospel through blogging and in the midst of it we will be called back to our land full of wealth which the Lord plans to give us through spreading the word of God.

Takeaway Tip: Seek the Lord about monetizing from your Christian Blog. Now that we know through the word of God that it is biblically ok to monetize through our ministry you must seek Him to know if this is the plan for your future. Answer these two questions then go to the Lord with a humble heart and be ready to receive the answer.

1. If you did start monetizing from your blog but then it all of a sudden stopped would you still bog?
2. Is your motive to blog to monetize?

– 12 –
Affiliate Marketing Part 1

Affiliate marketing was something that I was nervous to venture. I did not want to do affiliate marketing because I did not want to sound like a sales person (although I did have a successful ten year career in sales, I never wanted to be a "sales person") or be pushy in any way. I also did not want to just create posts for a product and the last impression I gave to readers was "Buy, Buy, Buy" I truly appreciate and honor my audience greater than a sales pitch.

By my third month I had signed up for a few affiliates that was recommended for new bloggers according to a mass amount of experienced bloggers. Shareasale and Amazon being amongst the list but had not yet used them by any extent that would generate an income.

In my fourth month of blogging my husband and I took the children on a road trip for our summer vacation. We had a bucket list of places we wanted to sightsee and visit. We figured we could do a road trip and see everything we were hoping to by driving up to Northern California to visit Yosemite National Park and San Francisco then drive the Pacific Coast Highway on our way back home. It was an exciting time but as we did this, it meant little access to WIFI and little time to work on the blog.

After several days of traveling we had arrived to a hotel that was not so rural on the PCH and I was finally able to open my laptop to decent WIFI. When I did, I opened up to a big surprise, my site 'Married by His Grace Blog' was down. I kept thinking it was the internet connection that was not responding even though my email came up perfectly. I had numerous emails unopened and among them was one from my hosting server stating they had to disable my site earlier that day due to terms of condition. I called the server and they told me my site had a high volume of activity and they had to disable due to call ins from other site owners because of interruptions to their site. As they were explaining this to me I looked at my analytics. My analytics showed that I had received over 4700 pageviews within the 10 hours that my site was up for that day. It was my first large amount of traffic to my blog.

One of my first written post "5 Things a Stay at Home Mom should do Everyday" went viral. (Viral is a term used of a post that rapidly grows in a short amount of time, whether it's by the amount of hundreds, thousands or millions). I was shocked, blessed, excited, and all of the above. My fourth month blogging and I had an amount of pageviews that any blogger hopes for in their journey. I spent two hours on the phone receiving assistance and adding a few plugins and then voila my site was up and running again. The next two weeks followed with close to 2,000 pageviews a day and a consistent amount of new Pinterest followers.

This experience gave me a big wakeup call as a "Business Owner". I had no affiliate marketing on my highest traffic page. I had google adsense and yes I was receiving an amount of revenue that I was never close to having before but there was nothing on my page to direct the stay at home moms to products that were related to the post.

Not only would adding Amazon as an affiliate marketing tool to the post would have been beneficial to me but would have added sensitivity to the readers. It would've been beneficial to the readers to be able to find a quick click to the items that was already freely recommended in the post. Needless to say, I learned a lot about how instantaneously it could feel like a loss but I also learned how I could improve it and how to create affiliate marketing posts without a fear of sounding too salesy or pushy.

As a blogger stay true in what you believe in and in the purpose of your blog. As your blog grows and you begin to venture out with affiliating it's important to not allow anything to interrupt your goals and visions.

Do not get overwhelmed with the thoughts that once you begin implementing affiliate marketing your blog will veer away from what God is doing. I was stuck in that mind set for a moment, and as I was stuck there I began losing the confidence in knowing that God is building a business for me to incorporate with His provision and Name written all over it. To avoid this happening to you pray for confidence if managing a business.

I am also a believer that we should be praying for the affiliates we plan to work with. To pray about the products we may represent. And to pray about the income of your blog. The income may not be but a few dollars but are you still willing to receive it with a heart of gratitude and content. The income may flourish high to more than you imagine but if the Lord requested for you to stop blogging as a business owner, would you continue to write for the effects of the kingdom and not your own? These are the things we will be asked from the Lord as we work with His word and His lead.

Takeaway Tip: Begin researching affiliates that you may be interested in. It's good practice to read their visions ahead of time so you will know if their visions are aligned with yours. Before officially joining an affiliate program that you already personally use; ask yourself, how will the products you choose benefit your audience and make them keep trust with you?

− 13 −

Affiliate Marketing Part 2

Questionnaire about affiliate marketing for the new blogger.

What is affiliate marketing?

Affiliate marketing is a partnership with another business or blogger that sells products. It involves you promoting a product on your blog or social media platforms. You will receive a commision when the potential buyer clicks on the link that you provided to direct them to the product. If a purchase is made, you will receive a commission anywhere between 1% to 50% of the sale. The percentage of commission depends on the program.

When a potential customer clicks on your link, there is usually an open window policy of how long till you can still receive a commission from the original click. For example if a reader clicks on a link I promoted on my blog but did not buy right away then the click is saved as a "cookie". If the same potential customer goes back to the affiliate site I had once referred them to within 30 days and purchases the product I would still gain a commission.

Should I do affiliate marketing?

I would say yes and yes over and over again to doing affiliate marketing as a blogger because it is a great source of income. It is known as one of the most popular ways to monetize for a blogger because it is a passive income. You can create one awesome post of a product and earn money consistently over time as traffic continues to go to that specific post. But I am also a big believer of using wisdom in all that you do as a representation of Christ and believe as Christian Bloggers, this is a decision that needs leading from God.

I do believe God is bringing many of us to a place that we will be able to make an income from a blog that is ministering to many souls out there but I also believe He has an appointed way of streamlining income for each and every one of us.

Although I participate in minimal affiliate marketing, this is not the streamline of income that the Lord is leading me to. When I realized that, I gave up a few affiliates I was promoting and now only use two which are ones that I prayed and researched about before choosing. The decision to follow the lead of the Lord proved itself it gave me peace of mind with my affiliates and contentment with the blogging income I now receive.

If you feel affiliate marketing would be a good match and you feel confident in this area to begin making an income. Then start wholeheartedly because although Affiliate Marketing is passive income, it also takes work and dedication to create a post that will lead to sales. .

Maybe the unction is not there to have Ads or affiliates on your site, maybe your blog posts are only to be filled with the words He has given you. Trust that He will show you what will be important and beneficial to your readers and how you can provide it. Affiliate Marketing is most effective when there is trust so it's important for us to use that character with our audience as we begin any type of streamlining of income from our blog.

How do I start partnering as an affiliate?

There are many companies for bloggers to affiliate with. To name just a few: Bluehost, Amazon, Etsy, Target, Starbucks,

Shareasale (numerous companies within) Tailwind, Connecting with Bloggers to sell their products, Website Template Developers and so forth.

You can literally go to any site that you would like to partner with and scroll down to the bottom of the site and can find an affiliate link, if offered. Once you click the affiliate link, majority of companies will have you read their requirements and policy to affiliating with them as a company. Some require a certain amount of pageview or a certain genre and topic within your site. All rules and regulation are different among companies.

Due to the least amount of regulations and wide range of selling opportunity of products, the most popular company to partner with as a blogger is Amazon. Amazon is simple to sign up with and is easy to use on your blog. Payout threshold is $100; meaning once you reach your $100 commission from them, you will then be paid out, if you do not reach their threshold by end of paid period (which is generally monthly) then it will roll over till you reach the $100 mark. There will be a different threshold on every company out there. Most are between a $50 to $100 payout.

What is the best way to start implementing on my blog that I am an affiliate?

When you are at least three to six months or over ten blog posts into blogging, my recommendation to figure out what would be best for your audience and stay in alignment with your blog is to go to your analytics, find your top 3-5 posts and ask yourself these two questions:

What do you think your readers liked most about it?
What product do you think would've matched up with that post?

Let's say your top post is about "Tools I use for Bible Studying" and you wrote about websites, bibles, and notebooks you use for studying the word, don't you think you could've added links back to those products that you already use and love? Your top post are top posts for a reason. Your readers love what you love and want to do what you do because they agree with you and trust you.

As you read earlier in the book affiliate marketing is something I learned the hard way because I was afraid to implement Affiliate Marketing due to looking salesy.

I already knew the '5 Things a Stay at Home Mom should do everyday' was my most viewed post but had not yet added any affiliates to it because of intimidation of trying something new and looking like a salesperson. A few days after the baby viral was beginning to die down a bit I finally added affiliate links that matched what I wrote about in the blog post and I saw immediate clicks to my affiliate links. When it went to receiving 2k views a day to 800 then to 500 a day, a lot of "what ifs" came to mind.

As a lesson learned on my behalf, I highly recommend starting with your most pageview posts when you begin implementing affiliate links.

Before doing this, by the Fair Trade Commission regulations you must add a Disclosure Policy to your blog that informs your readers that you use affiliate links and if they click on the link that you provide you may receive a small commission. It is wise to let your readers know that you only promote products that you personally use and believe in (which I hope you do). It is also best for you to list the affiliates that you are partnered with on your disclosure policy. You can place the disclosure policy by adding a page or category to your blogs site so it is separate from the rest of the blog.

When writing a post that involves affiliate links, it is best to also add on the post that "This post may contain affiliate links, please see my disclosure policy".

Many bloggers that make the majority of their income from Affiliate Marketing recommend adding affiliate links to EVERY post. I don't. Here's why: As a Christian Blogger we need to have discernment that some of our post are just for the cause of touching of His people. Certain posts are not to be of anything but filled with the Holy Spirit led words that came flowing through your hands onto the keyboard. God is first in all circumstances as a Christian writer and blogger and if discernment is telling you not to post affiliate links or anything else on a specific post then don't do it. Success of your blog is not measured by the likes, follows, or income, it's by the standards of following Christ.

Takeaway Tip: Create a draft of a Disclosure Policy for your blog. Disclosure policy is simple and usually of only one to two sentence. The policy is to give awareness to your readers that you may gain a commission from products and that you may earn an income from this promotion. Here is an example that I use:

"Married By His Grace is a blog that carefully chooses affiliates to work with. All companies and organizations on the site are ones that I believe and trust in. Any written post that offer compensation will be noted within posts."

– 14 –

Selling Products

There a few ways for a blogger to earn an income. Many bloggers will sell their own products and I will address the most common products individually. After going over the list of most well-known products that bloggers sell, it is best to create a pros and cons list before deciding which will be best for you to sell. Each of us will have our own list that is determined by what is best for us.

As a mom, an ebook was what I chose to do outside of Married by His Grace blog. Being able to write a book was first of all something I had a desire to do since a young age, being able to write based off of my own hours was compatible because I am a full time blogger, wife, mom, in ministry, and maintaining a home. I was not pressured with deadlines by others, only by my own self which is something I was able to change my mindset about if needed.

For others, writing a book may not be as compatible. Having to write content with a mass amount of words may be overwhelming or maybe writing a book is just not in your goals. But maybe using your creativity and selling printables is. Or creating webinars to train someone in an area that you are an expertise in may be your cup of tea (or coffee, whichever you prefer).

The suggestions I make may all sound good to you, but know that there is a bigger picture and a self-cost to each one. It's best to research the work and preparation needed to create the product. Knowledge is the key to open the doors of success.

Ebook - A digital book. Most common way of selling is through Amazon or through your own site. If you decide to sell on your own site I highly recommend to follow Abby Lawson from Just a girl and her blog. Her webinars and blog posts helped me tremendously while developing my own eBook.

Webinars - These can be done live or pre-recorded and sold as a training class for specific topics.

Digital Downloads - Anything your buyer can print on their own once they paid for the licensed graphic you created.

Calendars/Planners - Use your experience; use your testing and trials seasons to create printable calendars and planners for other bloggers, homeschooling moms, stay at home moms These are much appreciated by ones that are in search of this particular product. Being able to create detailed products through your experience makes it valuable and personal for the buyers.

E-course - Usually sold as pre-recorded. Sold in increments of a three, five, or a seven day course to learn about a specific topic you are an expertise in.

Services - Consulting, Freelance writing, Social Media Assistant. These are all services you can provide through your blog if it fits the needs of your readers.

Physical Products - Most common physical products that are made by bloggers is apparel, frame work, and jewelry. You can do this through having an Etsy shop, ecommerce (a digital shop you can create on your own site), or through a website such as Gumroad.

All the mentioned products may be known as popular products for bloggers to sell and a great place to start but the best products are the unique products.

Each of us have a passion and are most likely writing about it. Create a product that will describe your blog. Most likely the product you offer will sell to your readers and they will trust in what you write. Do not confuse them about selling a product that does not relate to your blog.

This is why it is important to know your audience before creating your product to ensure quality and success. Why do they visit your blog and what do they expect from you? What can you create to serve them with a purpose that they already appreciate from you and your blog?

To sell any of these products you will need to find a way to checkout with payment, how to receive the product and a site that can offer affiliate partners if this is something you would like to offer. The benefit of having a site such as Gumroad, Sendowl, or Shopify as a digital product check out is that you can give coupon codes, have early purchase program, and it's a five minute process to create your selling account.

With whatever product and or service you decide to do I hope your takeaway from this chapter is to consider all factors around you. Time, assistance, tools. Being a blogger is using wisdom in your capabilities to be able to maintain a blog and create new products that will require a high priority of attention to promote and sell.

Takeaway Tip: If your goal is to one day create a product or service for your audience, take time to write down your goal, give an estimated date of when you would like the product to launch. Write down the steps that will take you to achieve this. Statistics says if you write down a goal, you are 40% more likely to achieve it.

– 15 –

Staying Connected

Staying connected to your readers and followers should become a priority to you. Your readers are the ones that will keep encouraging you the moments you need it most. Most importantly your readers are the ones that are going to take you to the next level of blogging. People that follow your blog and subscribe to the blog follows you. As the creator and writer of the blog, you are the one that brings inspiration to them and they want to stay connected to it.

Recently I read a post about what a blogger has learned from her 1 year journey of blogging. Her statement "People over Projects" was so profound to me. The blogger explained "yes, as writers we need to be writing consistently and conducting our writing projects as the foundation of the blog but the readers and all the people involved is the core of our success for blogging."

If we continue to push back comments, personal emails, or interactions on social media with our readers than we are pushing back the backbone of the blog. A blog cannot stay afloat without them.

Reaching out and connecting with your readers keeps you in a place of humbleness. As your blog grows, humbleness will be a requirement. Humbleness is what will keep you connected with your readers and subscribers on an intimate level. Your writings can be amazing and look like the most professional blog out there but if you have no connection then you have nothing.

As the scripture tells us:

> *If I have the gift of prophecy, and know all mysteries and all knowledge; and if I have all faith, so as to remove mountains, but do not have love, I am nothing.*

> *1 Corinthians 13:2 NASB*

When I first started blogging, I would personally email readers that would leave their email address with a comment on my blog if it was something that touched my heart because they freely wrote a personal comment or even asked a question. My desire was to show how much their openness and comment meant to me by making a personal connection with them.

I almost always got a response and I have developed many beautiful relationships through this. I actually have also gained a blogging best friend through a personal email I sent in response to a comment. We now lead a private Facebook group together and share a lot of our blogging experiences together. It has been a tremendous blessing to me.

I still continue to do this when a new reader leaves a comment and I receive many flattering emails of appreciation that I emailed them personally and this brings absolute joy to me. I love connecting with others on a different level. My desire is to become intimate with others through the relationship of Christ in our lives and by reaching out to them individually this has increased my faith in what God is calling me to through Married by His Grace blog.

Connecting with your readers is not only a relationship through your blog but you can also create rapport with your audience through social media. Comment back when they comment on any of your posts on Instagram, Facebook, Twitter. Like their comment. Let them see that you saw them.

Just as I stated from the the beginning the blog is not only about you, it's about them. Do not respond to their comments or like with only making it about you. Engage with them, with who they are. Learning more about them teaches you about your demographics. Who is reading you blog or following you on social media? What is it that they like about your postings and writings? What else can you do to help your audience?

Connecting with your readers builds relationships and is a learning tool. Receive the benefits of this.

Takeaway Tip: Begin a habit of responding to your readers on your blog and your social media platforms. Take time to personally email recent comments on your blog from readers that touched your heart or that was seeking further detail about your post.

– 16 –

Networking

Besides writing, networking has become one of my favorite parts of blogging. I have been blessed and honored to meet so many amazing bloggers that are passionately spreading the word of God through their writings.

Besides developing Christ like relationships, networking has been a tremendous help to the building of my blog for several reasons.

- I have developed relationships with other bloggers who are able and willing to teach us in all areas of blogging..
- The Blogger Community supports one another by sharing others content and promos.
- Encouragement from other bloggers in my niche has stopped me from giving up on blogging several times.
- I have received invites to group boards and private groups that have contributed to enlarging my audience.
- I have been asked to do guest posting because of an already built relationship with another blogger.
- I have been able to find guest bloggers for my blog by bloggers that I trust with the same beliefs and views as I have.
- It keeps me from forgetting I am not alone.
- The unity with other bloggers keeps me humble.

Networking is important to do for all of the above reasons and for more reasons that you will learn through experiencing networking.

Ways you can network with other bloggers is by joining Facebook groups, Link Parties, and Pinterest boards. Creating your own Facebook group would also be a step in the right direction of networking.

Look to join or create a Facebook group that has the same visions and goals as your blog. When you do this you put yourself in the position to gain knowledge, insight, and encouragement that will help you in your blogging journey.

One of my top favorite ways is network is through Link Parties. The Arabah Joy and Raising Homemakers blogs host Link Parties that I participate in consistently. Link Parties generally go live once a week for 1 day (24 hours). You can join by adding your blog link to the designated area on the post. When you upload your blog link, you will be able to share your most recent post. Other bloggers and readers will click on the image that was uploaded from your blog site and will be referred to the post. Just like how it would work if you posted a link in Facebook or Pinterest; it will show the image but not the post.

The way Link Parties become a good way of networking is that hosts will set rules and guidelines that if you leave your link for others to visit you must visit two or more other posts within the Link Party and leave a positive comment. The person that leaves a positive comment usually leaves a note that they had found you through the Link Party and they too are a blogger. This is when I like to reach out and visit their site also to leave a positive comment. I have developed great blogging friendships through this.

The benefits of joining support and network groups for bloggers is valuable.

Takeaway Tip: Join Link Parties. You can find Link Parties through other blog sites, through Pinterest, or Bloggers sharing about them in Blogging Facebook Groups. I participate in Arabah Joy's Link Party which is every Friday and Raising Homemakers, every Wednesday.

− 17 −

Handling Discouragement in Blogging

Christian Bloggers, I decided to end this book on the chapter of 'Handling Discouragement in Blogging', not because the title itself sounds a little weary and I did not want to scare you off in the beginning but because the cold true fact of it, is that just like this is the last chapter, the discouragement will be one of the last things that will try to creep in as you begin to start your blog and new business adventure.

The common steps of starting a new venture:

1. Vision - Bringing life to your niche.

2. Excitement - You cannot stop thinking about the new adventure you are about to begin.

3. Researching - Knowledge is key.

4. Preparation - No time for emotions.

5. Ready to start - Excitement builds up again and you are feeling a handful of emotions but overall the excitement of a new beginning is at its highest point.

6. A hit in your confidence - But with one talk from a supporter, you are ready to go again. This can be confused with discouragement but often this comes from lack of sleep and motivation due to moving rapidly when starting a blog/business.

7. You receive a rewarding feeling of Completion - You have officially launched!

8. Excitement strikes again - The visions you began with are again arising and reminding you of the soon to be great success.

9. Boom - Hit by discouragement out of nowhere. The supporter is on extra duty.

10. You overcome.

I write this out to you step by step in hopes that you realize, **You Are Not Alone**. Bloggers will get discouraged. Christian bloggers will get even more discouraged whether because technical difficulty makes you feel overwhelmed, numbers are not growing like you had hoped, or that one comment about on social media made you question if people really like your blog.

There can be a multitudes of reasons for discouragement when blogging but there needs to be a point, before the point of no return, when to bring it all back to why you started - not because you wanted to make an extra income or create a following, as stated before in the book. If you're not sure of the reason for starting or if this is really God leading you then you will not be able to continue leading your blog where it is supposed to go.

You have to be confident that the blog you created was by the leading of the Lord and you must take it back to Him every time you are discouraged.

Truth is, as a Christian blogger we are developing a ministry that is a representation of who Christ is within us. The moment you declare who you are in Christ is the moment you can fulfill what the Lord is requesting for you to do.

Walk with confidence of who you are in Christ in this journey. Walk with accountability and maturity. Your calling requires it. Thankfully the simplicity of being able to do this is by staying connected with the Lord.

Dear Lord,
I pray for wisdom, clarity, patience, and humbleness over myself and my fellow Christian Bloggers. I ask for you to keep us stirred up with boldness and courage to accomplish the plans you have set before us. I pray we keep obedience to You as we write Your words. That the leading of our hand is only through you. May our hearts be passionate to reach your people with the boldness of spreading the gospel. Give us insight to what you hope for us to accomplish. May we stay diligent and true to it. Bless each of our fellow bloggers with hope, encouragement, and grace. We pray for Your Name to continue being greater than any other name. As we speak from nation to nation through writing, may the words not be oppressive but be full of mercy and grace. In Jesus name, with much honor unto our King, Amen.

Until I come, devote yourself to the public reading of Scripture, to exhortation, to teaching. Do not neglect the gift you have...'

1 Timothy 4:13-14 ESV

Takeaway Tip: Enjoy your blogging journey!

Thank you for completing *By His Grace We Blog: The Perfect Resource for the Christian Blogger*. I hope you have found it to be encouraging, resourceful, and a full of insight that can assist you in your blogging journey in the Christian niche.

For more content regarding Christian Blogging, you may visit Married by His Grace.

Made in the USA
Middletown, DE
09 February 2019